the texts that never delivered.

alysha patel

51

messages

undelivered.

contents

chapter 1

disconnected.

erupted.

did i really hurt you that bad, that
i am the one to suffer now?

our love was once heavenly, and now i
feel the regret seeping through my
body…

a body is known as one's temple, so
why does mine burn like hell?

the anger races through my veins like
a volcano ready to erupt.

evil.

you built a foundation of love and
growth to only be the destroyer.

we built an empire; you were my
emperor... you became my enemy and
all evil to ever exist.

lifeless love.

i just wanted our love to continue
like the endless tides, but instead
my heart sunk, and we

d

r

o

w

n

e

d

bystander.

our love sailed through storms, but
you ended up being the passing
hurricane that i should have never
met with.

thoughts.

i allowed myself to fall into this
deep infatuation, knowing there could
never be a happily ever after with a
person who's stuck in the past.

wasted.

i want your love, but do not want my
time to be wasted. i want to love
you, but do not want my love to be
wasted.

saviour.

you saved me out of love like a
saviour, but in the end all it felt
like was a favour.

you were a deadly sinner, our love
turned to catastrophe, what a sight
that was to see.

you left me like a lifeless body, no
remorse nor a sorry.

misunderstood love.

you taught me how to love, but you
never taught me what love felt like…

the difference between the two is you
walked away as if nothing happened,
while i had to pick up the pieces to
a heart i didn't break...

volume.

your voice was like a song i could
not stop listening to, your words
were lyrics i could not forget.

i d a n c e d to your tune even after
you were gone.

drift.

people say ‘**slow and steady wins the race**’...

but we went so s l o w l y⌐ you drifted away from me⌐ like a leaf⌐ steadily falling to the ground⌐ crumbling as the seasons passed.

the one person to win this race was you⌐ with someone else.

lost in your fire.

our love became a blazing s

p

i

r

a

l

you started a fire in my heart that
no amount of water could put out, and
nobody could stop.

mind over matter.

i could sit and try describing the
pain of losing what i thought was the
love of my life, but no words could
ever express the shadows of doubt, or
pain that overtakes my mind every
time someone mentions your name.

chapter 2

the unsent and unsaid.

scenario.

i am floating between reality and worst-case scenario.

i am sat thinking about overthinking, as i try to figure out my state of mind.

i realise my mind will not stray away from the thoughts of you.

am i daydreaming? or is this my new reality after losing you?

heart strings.mp3.

you told me to always face the music,
but the only music you wanted to play
was my heart strings.

you walked away with all the beats
and rhythm it had left.

burning desires.

the desire to love you is stronger
than my willpower to leave you. i'd
rather be hurting with you, than
without.

the love risk.

love is passion,

obsession

&

raw emotion

to love is a challenge, opportunity,
and experience everyone must live…

because to have never loved at all is
a life unfulfilled, full of regret &
loneliness.

l o n g i n g.

i   long   for   love   that   won't
die, friendships that   will   remain
and   memories   that   don't   fade.

lifeline.

love is what keeps people going,

love should be shared and cherished,

love is like the air we breathe every
single day.

without it we would all be dead.

borrowed time.

you were my lover by choice… but not
mine as such, as my heart decided
that.

your love took me places i never
thought i would discover and made me
feel a way i never thought i could.

but i guess that is the ending to a
not so happily ever after fairy tale.

as you left my mind lost in the
confusion of your love.

deadly lies.

you said you would be dead without
me, but you are the one still
breathing... not me, *you*.

poetic mind.

everything written and revised is
poetry when your heart aches, mind
overloads, and darkness clouds your
judgement.

ego.

vanity is an ego killer.

you wanted to work on yourself but
left for someone else?

surely that's just selfishness.

continuous.

with you i was either dreaming or
working.

the meanings are not the same, in
fact they are opposites just like us.

but either way i remained optimistic
with our dreamy scheduled
relationship.

the last assignment.

i could write a dissertation on our
love, but no amount of words could
describe the way you made me feel.

moving on.

i should be happy for you, cause all
i ever wanted was your happiness, so
why do i feel emotionless?

you moved on without any hesitation,
any remorse and no *'i'm sorry'* or no,
'one more time' you have been holding
someone else, while i have been
holding on by a thread.

loving you.

you saw the sky as blue on days i saw
it as grey. you were like this gift
from god i never believed could be
real.

i loved you with every bone in my
body, every breath from my lungs,
every pump of blood i had left.

you showed me direction in my life,
results to a purposeful life, you
made every day worth living, every
step worth 100 more, hand in hand
'forever&always' you said.

chapter 3

low battery.

goodbye.

you left…

why did you leave?

if our eyes did not meet like sinners
in hell, would we still be the best
of friends living in our heaven?

were we meant for each other, or did
we kid ourselves?

did you ever love me, or were you the
poison my veins needed to suffice in
this dark world?

race my mind.

my mind is always r a c i n g,

you seem to be the driver, but i
guess our love was a race against
time since we crashed, and you left
me to burn down.

past tense.

all the hidden words within the
conversations we never got to have,
to every passive aggressive
conversation, to no sound at all.

strangers we now become in volumes of
miscommunication.

communication.

was communication really our thing?

how about actions?

see because, i could never truly show
you how much i loved you, because in
my eyes no gift, no sense of words in
the dictionary were ever going to
truly be good enough.

but that is just the problem.

'words'- due to the lack of them we
are now strangers.

strangers in a world we once were
lovers.

all these 'what if's' continue to
stab me in the mind like a blunt
sword.

o v e r.

from loving

to arguing,

to making up,

to enough is enough you are dead to
me.

we are strangers but not by
choice...well my choice anyway.

half ~~dead.~~

(n.) heartbreak is what it's called
so why do i feel half dead?

it's as if i was shot in the heart by
your love, wounded with the memories
of you and left with a hole of
bleakness i now have to walk around
with.

selfish.

would things be different right now
if we spoke more?

if we got together later, would we
have been happier?

so many unanswered questions, yet so
many filled silences.

your silence really did speak higher
volumes, you left without a look
back.

you promised to be cautious of my
heart and i promised to never hurt
yours.

all these empty promises led to the
brutal breakup and our break down.

physical broken bones to an
indescribable broken mind.

i felt as if the world had crumbled,

i felt as if i died everyday again
and again until reality hit... you
really did leave and i must carry on,
i must be selfish again.

ace of spades.

you dealt me the deck of cards,

gave me your heart and our love was ace.

you ruled like a king, called me your queen…

yet i left as the joker.

prisoner.

a prisoner i am to your love,
imprisoned by my own thoughts of you.
i try to escape day in, day out.
death row seems easier than
forgetting you.

wicked games.

i was told playing with fire would
get me burnt, but why did nobody warn
me about the game of love and how it
destroys every last bit of you.

search & rescue.

you left to find something better,
but what's better than someone who'd
lose their life for you in a
heartbeat?

~~undelivered.~~

all the things we left unsaid are all
the things you did with someone else.

chapter 4

out of storage.

for you.

for all you did, for who you are
always, i will be forever grateful
you were in my life and left me with
some gracious memories.

summer szn.

your love felt like endless summers.

starry eyed.

the sparks of our love flew greater
and further.

your eyes when you used to look at me
created a gentle explosion of love.

before i knew it there was a showcase
of fireworks.

spoken, signed & sealed.

the quiet chaos of your lips as you
uttered my name, never felt the same
from that day on as it became yours
to claim.

platform edge.

it was the lump in the back of my
throat when i would have to leave
you, the lonesome wonder to the
platform departing from you,
wondering when the next time will be
until our souls collide again.

a dozen cuts.

i won't wait to give you your
flowers, you deserve a dozen roses…

but roses have their thorns just like
you had the power to cut me with your
sharp words.

devil in disguise.

love at first sight? i'd say so.

forever was in your eyes and your smile guided me through our darkest days and toughest nights. i knew i wanted to be the reason for your smile forever.

&

even though we may not be together, i hope you smile with the same innocence & purity that made you- my weakness.

too much too late.

people say the hardest pill to
swallow is walking away…

but the hardest part of it all was
trying to free my mind of you, and
disconnect my heart of all the
emotions and love i felt for you.

i guess it's too much too late, to
say the least.

love & war.

falling for you was the most out of
body experience. i always thought
we'd be forever, but now i have love
wounds to prove i fought this battle
long and hard.

oh, and in case you are wondering...
wounds heal so i won against the war
of heartbreak.

seasonal high.

you were my summer, it was never
about the sunshine, laughter, or
adventures, it was all **you.** every
passing day mattered cause they were
spent with my sunshine...**you.**

act 4, scene 11.

it's said true love is only for the
books, films & plays, but between the
lines of our love i found god's most
precious creation…

the character played by you.

ghost.

your love made me feel like the world
was on pause…

…

…

…

nothing else mattered.

nobody else mattered.

nothing could ruin our time, our
bond, and our love.

you made me feel invincible but
really, i was just invisible to you.

reality.

nonetheless, with all the moments we
shared, our love is out of my hands.

it deserves freedom from my mind,
because it's a choice i cannot
control, and a consequence i need to
accept.

isbn: 9798860447677

imprint: independently published by amazon.

editor: eesha patel

art director/designer: riya patel

production editor: riya patel

contributions by: alisha bharmal

Printed in Great Britain
by Amazon